60 ²

Antonio Mirabal
1931

Oil, 20″ x 16″

Private Collection

Maynard Dixon

Images of the Native American

The California Academy of Sciences
San Francisco

This book has been set in Goudy Old Style type and printed
on 100 lbs, matte coated New Age Book.

Design Michael Vanderbyl

Production Piper Murakami

Printed in Japan through Interprint, San Francisco

Table of Contents

List of Plates

Dedication

This catalogue, which complements an exhibition of major works by a great California painter, Maynard Dixon, salutes the achievements of another distinguished California citizen, George Edmund Lindsay. George retires from the demanding job as Director of the California Academy of Sciences in August 1981, after eighteen extraordinary years of service to this institution.

George has vigorously led the institution forward and leaves behind him a natural history museum and research facility of national renown.

George has been supported by a truly remarkable woman, his lovely wife, Geraldine Kendrick Lindsay. We appreciate and recognize her continuing efforts on the Academy's behalf.

We thank you, George and Gerry Lindsay, for your dedication to excellence and for your grand vision.

Paul L. Davies, Jr.

Buffalo Dance
1931

Ink and Crayon, 5⅝″ x 6⅛″

Collection of Edith Hamlin

Foreward

Maynard Dixon was an artist, poet, Bohemian, admirer and interpreter of the West and the Native Americans who lived there. That latter interest, and the coincidence that Edith Hamlin, Donald J. Hagerty, and Kirsten and Peter Bedford share an association with the California Academy of Sciences, resulted in this major exhibition of Maynard Dixon's work. It is appropriate that it be presented at the Academy, which in recent years has developed diverse displays and programs honoring American Indians and has become a repository for their cultural and artistic treasures.

Academy Trustee Peter B. Bedford sponsored the exhibition, and Kirsten Bedford encouraged and coordinated its development. Their generous interest made it possible.

I want also to thank Edith Hamlin, widow of the artist, for her early and continuing encouragement and involvement, and for allowing us to use Maynard Dixon's personal records. The Dixon family, Constance, Daniel, and John, along with two close friends, Ansel Adams and Winona Tomanoczy, joined Edith in sharing their personal recollections which add richness to this catalogue.

I feel most fortunate that Donald J. Hagerty, who has studied Dixon for many years, gave us the important biography and information about the development of Dixon's empathy and esteem for the Indians with whom he lived.

We have received invaluable assistance from museums, private collectors, and art dealers. Special thanks are deserved by Dr. Joseph Baird for his editorial advice, Howard Willoughby for his knowledge and help, the staffs of numerous institutions for their cooperation and support—Eugene Adkins, Jack Burke, Steve Good, Richard Hilligass, Frank Snell, and others unacknowledged in the catalogue text.

To all who have worked so creatively on this catalogue and exhibit, we express our gratitude.

George Lindsay

Baldwin Murals
Envoys of Peace (top)
Victory Song (bottom)
1913

Oil, 48″ x 216″

Private Collection

Visions and Images: Maynard Dixon and the American West
Donald J. Hagerty

Among the many artists who have sought to interpret the spirit, character and life of that section of our country known as the American West, few have succeeded as well or as completely as Maynard Dixon. Numerous elements in the frontier West have served for both American history and art. The land which beckoned beyond the Mississippi, the natives of the Plains, the Southwest, and the Rockies, the evolving frontiers from gold bonanzas to cattle empires were subjects that fascinated countless Americans. These and countless more Western themes became pervasive elements in American literature and art. The Western frontier created images assimilable nationally as cultural pattern.[1] Maynard Dixon both interpreted and contributed to this cultural pattern.

Lafayette Maynard Dixon was born January 24, 1875, in the raw and energetic frontier town of Fresno, California. His father, Harry St. John Dixon, had fought for the Confederacy during the Civil War. His mother, Constance, had migrated West before the war. As a young and sensitive child, his first impressions of the San Joaquin Valley were of a prairie with a few ranches, houses, and barns, standing like islands in a sea. Always in view were the rugged blue and white walls of the Sierra Nevada. From arroyo and slough to the new railroad line, the irrigation ditches, and fences separating the vast cattle ranches—everywhere was a dead level, with a horizon that radiated toward a clear blue dome from the town whose lone water tank appeared to be exactly in the center.[2]

Equally strong and enduring influences on young and imaginative Dixon came from the people of the area. Fresno was a boom town fueled by land and water speculators, new settlers, and other people attracted to a new frontier. The atmosphere was a cultural continuation from the Gold Rush era. Long-haired men were still in evidence and Rocky Mountain trappers, cattlemen, miners, and adventure seekers of the previous generation abounded here and in many California towns. The sensitive and keenly observant boy was impressed by the stark essentials—the big bones and long lines in the landscape and people, bare of any unnecessary padding. Dixon never forgot these early influences of an unadorned expansiveness of country and strong character of people. They dominate and give an unmistakable signature to his drawings, canvases, murals, and poetry.

Trips into the High Sierrra, to the remote wilderness of the Kern River and Kaweah Range, increased Dixon's interest in the world around him. He never forgot the aesthetic power of the few surviving Mono Indians moving across the horizon. This vision—man's relationship to the earth—is seen in many of Dixon's important later works. Solitary rides on horseback around Fresno, observing and sketching, and the reading of *Harper's Magazine*, *Scribner's*, and the *Art Journal* with their illustrations by Howard Pyle, Frederic Remington, and others, were sources for his increasing interest and proficiency in drawing.

In 1891, Dixon's father suffered a nervous breakdown, and the family moved to Coronado where Dixon did studies of the old adobes of San Diego and nearby towns with their remnants of Spanish and Mexican cultures. During the same year, at the age of sixteen, Dixon determined to devote his life to illustrating the Old West. He sent two of his sketchbooks to Frederic Remington, who responded with encouraging criticism. That encouragement sent him forth on his personal and professional odyssey.

Dixon moved to San Francisco in 1892 and continued to develop his drawing during 1893 and 1894 by making sketches in his neighborhood, on trips to "Refuge," the Dixon ranch near Fresno, on horseback rides into Yosemite, and while camping with Portuguese and Mono Indian sheepherders. By 1895, he was contributing illustrations to the *Overland Monthly* and the San Francisco *Morning Call* and *Examiner*. From 1895 to 1899, Dixon wrote articles and provided numerous illustrations on Western life and people; among them he illustrated Jack London's Alaska stories in the *Overland Monthly*. He went on sketching trips to the Delta around Stockton and Union Island, up to the Mother Lode, and down to Monterey and the Big Sur country. About this time Dixon began to write poetry and to express himself through the written word with the same vigor and individuality we see in his art. Poetry would serve as Dixon's companion through personal and artistic travails, and as verbal articulation to his artistic work.

An early and major influence on Dixon's direction was Charles F. Lummis. Lummis published a magazine in Los Angeles, *Land of Sunshine*, from 1894 to 1909, which promoted Southwestern regionalism. Dixon illustrated a number of articles in this magazine, and he and Lummis became life-time friends. Dixon credited "Pop" Lummis with having been one of the two or three people whose advice and ideas had a strong impact upon his artistic life. Lummis was an enormously enthusiastic interpreter of the Southwest. He gathered a large following out of sheer exuberance, incessant activity, and undying fascination for "the Southwest," a term which he helped to popularize. In 1897, Lummis published some of Dixon's early attempts at verse and encouraged him to link poetry with his art. It was undoubtedly Lummis who urged Dixon to visit the Southwest.

In the early summer of 1900, Dixon crossed the Colorado River at Needles, leaving a temporal home and entering a spirtual home important in a struggle to express his personal vision. This first trip into the Southwest established irrevocably the development of Dixon's major themes in his work—the Native American and Western landscape. Dixon sketched Mojave Indians around Needles, Fort Mojave and Roberts Ranch, and traveled on to Prescott and the cattle ranges of the Aqua Fria Valley. His impressions of Phoenix were of adobe buildings, wagons, buggies, and saddled horses tied before wide awnings. Pima, Papago, and Maricopa Indians, arrayed in gay silks and calicos, dotted the sidewalks; there was the sizable if not important "Chihuahua Town,"

Medicine Woman
1920

Oil, 42″ x 62″

Courtesy of Hunter Gallery
San Francisco

The Wise Men
1923

Oil, 36″ x 40″

Collection of John E. Dixon

as Dixon termed it. Impressions of Arizona were to leave lasting memories. Dixon long remembered his first desert camp at Sacaton on the Pima Reservation:

Here I first met the saguaro. Close to my bed stood the tall shaft of one devoid of branches. All that long sleepless night it dominated me, a dark finger of doubt pointing ominously forever into an unknowable universe of stars. [3]

After absorbing the flavor of life around Tempe, Dixon went to the Verde Valley, explored the cream colored cliffs around the cliff dwelling of Montezuma's Castle, and dreamed of a far and forgotten past. He felt that the dim Indian ghosts he imagined befriended him:

I knew them again at old Oraibi, at Walpi, at Mishongnovi, at Shipaulovi and at silent Betatakin — and through them I have reached to something I cannot name, yet more than half believe. Somehow, it seems you may not understand Indians until you make friends with the ghosts. [4]

Dixon went on to the pueblo of Isleta, New Mexico where he had agreed to meet Charles Lummis. For many weeks he lived in the home of one of the pueblo leaders, Juan Rey Abeita, his sympathy and understanding for the people growing. He then returned to San Francisco to become one of the illustrators of the San Francisco Sunday *Examiner* as well as to illustrate magazine articles and a few books. Back in San Francisco, he was haunted by the urge "to go out."

Accompanied by his friend Edward Borein, later to become a noted Western artist, Dixon headed north in 1901—covering over a thousand zigzag miles of rough country through cattle ranches in Lassen and Modoc counties and out through the gray landscape of sage and mountain ranges of Southeastern Oregon to Boise, Idaho. Returning home, he summed up the trip as "plenty of sketches, no oils, new knowledge of Indians, and cowboy and range life in a tough country, and a greater respect for facts." Some of Dixon's illustrations of cowboy life were published several times on the covers of *Harper's Weekly* in 1902.

In 1902, Dixon again headed for Arizona. From Winslow, he headed north for the Hopi country. At Oraibi, he sketched the village, the Hopi, a Snake Dance, and the Navajo policemen. He went on to Polacca and Walpi and over to Ganado where he stayed with Lorenzo Hubbell and made numerous sketches of the Navajo around the trading post. There were over 30,000 Navajo, Dixon was told, in the surrounding vastness of mesas, plains, and canyons, which no white man knew. To a man on horseback or in a wagon the world was on a large scale—and roads were trails or wagon tracks. Dixon sketched everything he saw, and in later years returned often to Navajo country. He was deeply moved by what he saw:

Navajoland appears as a great empty place, decorated with a scattering of curious names: Jeditoh Springs, Skeleton Mesa, Canyon del Muerto, Aga-thla Needle, Nach-tee Canyon, Monument Valley, the Mittens, Pei-ki-hat-tsoh Wash—all hinting a far strangeness. A vast and lonely land it is, saturated with inexhaustible sunlight and astounding color, visible with unbelievable distinctness, and overspread with intense and infinite blue. Its long drawn levels are a setting for the awesome pageant of gigantic storms advancing under sky-built domes of clouds, trailing curtains of rain and thin color-essence of rainbows.

This is the land of mesas, laid down in layers of colored sandstone, red, yellow, pink and creamy white; carved and hollowed by the recession of forgotten seas; their sides often sheer, or broken into strange isolated slabs, turrets, buttes—the blind blunt architecture of a pre-human world. Afar they dwindle away, small and sharp, into clear blue distance and stop short; or in the long yellow slant of late sun their intricate forms are revealed in bewildering patterns of shadow; or seen only as low-lying bands of purple or sombre blue, remote in the shadow of rain clouds. [5]

Additional trips to the Southwest and a trip to Guadalajara, Mexico, in 1905, with fellow artist Xavier Martínez followed. At this period his pen and ink and pencil drawing techniques were being strengthened by his study of the German Art periodicals *Jugend* and *Simplicissimus*.

By 1905, Dixon had become an established illustrator. His illustrations were, and are today, vivid pictures of a changing frontier and its life of action—of men on the ranges, roundups, plunging horses in the dust-laden air of corrals, scenes in the streets of raw frontier towns, gambling halls, saloons, trading posts, lonely ranches, and Indian camps. Dixon's work appeared numerous times on covers and in articles for *Sunset, Pacific Monthly,* and other periodicals and for the San Francisco *Chronicle* and *Bulletin*. Occasional attempts at painting produced Post-Impressionist-like works such as *Old Apache, Moqui Town Crier, In Navajo Land,* and *Recuerdo de Guadalajara*. His first major exhibition, at the Bohemian Club in 1905, brought him recognition as a painter when James D. Phelan, later a United States Senator, purchased one of his pictures. Dixon's association with the Bohemian Club, which was to last until 1930, was a natural outlet for his iconoclastic, colorful, and occasionally irreverent personality. He counted among his fellow Bohemian friends such individuals as George Sterling, Arnold Genthe, Xavier Martínez, Robert Aitken, Porter Garnett, Will Irwin, and other noted artistic and literary figures.

The April 1906 earthquake and fire destroyed Dixon's studio, from which he was able only to rescue a few sketches and Navajo blankets. Like many other San Francisco artists and writers, Dixon headed for New York; with him was his new wife, Lillian West Tobey. Funds for the trip were provided by his first commission for a mural, one he did for the Southern Pacific's Tucson office. Dixon spent five uneasy years in New York's "boiling multitude." He became one of the

Pony Boy
1920

Oil, 36″ x 72″

Collection of Katherine H. Haley

The Ancients
1922

Oil, 25″ x 30″

Collection of Mrs. Frank Brophy

most successful of the book and magazine illustrators, in an era considered the "golden age of illustration." *Harper's Weekly, Scribner's, Century, Collier's, McClure's, Munsey's,* and other magazines illustrated Western adventure stories with Dixon's work. He also illustrated Western novels, including Clarence Mulford's *Hopalong Cassidy* stories and books by a fellow Westerner, Dane Coolidge. His work followed along the tradition of realistic illustrations of the period.

Dixon did not enjoy his New York illustrator's life. It made him money, but it forced him to present the West in a melodramatic, commercialized image of life there. Nevertheless he was gaining increased recognition. Two color canvases were accepted in 1910 by the National Academy of Design, and he was elected to membership in the Architectural League, the Salamagundi Club, and the New York Society of Illustrators. Another important event that occurred in 1910 was the birth of his daughter, Constance. Frequenters of Dixon's studio were Charles M. Russell, Edward Borein, Eugene Manlove Rhodes, Dane Coolidge, Will James, Indian models such as Tahamont (Dark Cloud), an Abenaki from Maine, and other well-known authors and illustrators of the day.

Dixon's only relief from the East was a trip to Northern Idaho and Montana in 1909 to study the Nez Perce, Flathead, and Blackfoot Indians and to visit old-timers. His New York life was beginning to exact its toll. Dixon remarked in a letter to Dane Coolidge that, "This last winter has sure put us on the blink, and I don't think we can stand another season of this country without going altogether stale." His dispirited and caustic view of the city's hectic life is reflected in one of his poems, *Quest* (c. 1910):

Through the noisy and mocking city
Amid turmoil distraction and clamor
Asking what God is . . .

Power and Force —
Smoke-giants and steam — electricity
Machinery, engines and steel,
The threatening glow of their fires,
din and confusion,
Millions of people, pouring over and over,
Rushing, crowding, contending . . .

Do I see hope in their eyes,
Asking what God is? [6]

Dixon came to an important decision in 1912. He would return to San Francisco and the West where "he could do honest work."

The year 1912 was a turning point in Dixon's life. In that year Anita Baldwin McClaughry, daughter of Nevada silver-millionaire, E. J. "Lucky" Baldwin, commissioned Dixon to paint a series of wall murals in her Sierra Madre home near Pasadena. It was Anita Baldwin who gave Dixon the opportunity to do major mural work. The murals—*Victory Song, Envoys of Peace, (pages 10, 11), The Pool,* and *Ghost Eagle.* —depicted Indian subjects and won critical acclaim for Dixon from the Los Angeles *Times,* San Francisco *Chronicle,* and such art magazines as *International Studio.* He emphasized the idea that the murals were intended to suggest rather than depict the life of Plains Indians. Dixon, a master storyteller as a muralist, would later write in 1925:

There is, after all, an American rhythm, and we are undoubtedly becoming more aware of it. And I believe that Daniel Boone, Andrew Jackson, Kit Carson, Abe Lincoln, P.T. Barnum and Henry Ford are manifestations of it no less than Walt Whitman, Edgar Lee Masters, Winslow Homer, Geo. Bellows and Rockwell Kent are expressions of it, that the transcontinental migration of 1841-68 was part of it in the same sense that our railway development is part of it; and that the suggestion of decorative art and a touch of mysticism that we have absorbed from the Amerindians is also a part.

I believe, further, that one of the most important ways in which system may be expressed for the people is through the decoration of public buildings, that through interpreting subjects of American history and American conditions in our own temper we may develop an American expression. [7]

Dixon returned to San Francisco, moved into the Osborne House on Russian Hill (where Mrs. Robert Louis Stevenson had stayed) and took refuge working furiously on easel painting. The years 1915 to 1919 were personally trying ones due to an increasingly strained marriage, and Dixon's view that the West as he knew it was being "finished by Henry Ford, the movies, dude ranches, and show business." He knew he was witnessing the end of an era. He credited the Panama-Pacific International Exposition of 1915 with a healthful revision of his ideas on color and space relations. One of his canvases, *The Trail in Oregon,* won the bronze medal. Another canvas, *Corral Dust,* was purchased by the M. H. de Young Museum. In 1916, Dixon joined the commercial art company of Foster and Kleiser and worked until 1921 producing striking billboard posters and other designs in color. He credited this work as excellent preparation for mural decoration. "It gave me," Dixon explained, "new experience in design and color, and attention value."

In 1917, Louis W. Hill, President of the Great Northern Railway, commissioned Dixon to do a group of paintings featuring Glacier National Park and the Blackfoot Indians—the Great

Mystery Stone
1922

Oil, 30″ x 25″

Private Collection

Tradition
1922-29

Oil, 30″ x 40″

Private Collection

Northern's principal tourist attractions. Taking his six year old daughter, Constance, with him, Dixon joined Frank Hoffman, a well-known illustrator, and spent August, September, and October of 1917 camping and painting in the clear, crisp autumn weather. Here Dixon renewed his acquaintance with Charles M. Russell, whom he had met during his New York period. Results of this trip included such outstanding paintings as *Medicine Woman (page 14)*, *Blackfeet Historians*, *The Story Tellers*, and many drawings.

By 1919, in the world of art, neither Dixon's former achievements nor the new fashions satisfied him. "Modernism" was rapidly gaining adherents and recognition, yet he found little that could be made to correspond to his own perceptions, his own honest vision. For Dixon, however free the emotional interpretation of things observed or experienced, that interpretation must contain a common denominator of human values.

By 1920, Dixon had worked out techniques to express the Old West as he felt it had to be and discovered that it was changing under the impact of popular culture. Henry Ford and the movies had taken the Old West away. The inexpensive automobile had destroyed the isolation of the small communities, and the movies had made the cowboys self-conscious. The motion picture began by imitating the Old West, and the Old West then began imitating the movies. The Old West was going, and the New West had not yet arrived. This development evidently began to shift Dixon's perceptions from a romantic and historical interpretation to a more psychological approach to his work. According to Dixon's widow, Edith Hamlin:

Dixon's fluency with drawing in every medium, pencil, pen and ink, crayon and charcoal, formed a secure basis for all of his later creations. His work is readily recognizable for its expressive and rhythmic line and the masterful drawing quality. After 1913, with his return from New York to the West, he was able to concentrate on both easel painting and murals, which allowed his facile illustrative draftsmanship to develop in more expressive and creative directions. From spontaneous, rather impressionistic oil paintings from the 1900s to the early 1920s, he evolved a flatter surface treatment with a bolder composition that was more simplified and geometric. By the 1930s, he included what he called "space division" in order to bring into line the most dominant diagonals, horizontals or verticals of his work. In both field drawings as well as studio compositions and landscapes, Dixon was very selective as to the simplification of the subject material—rearranging, discarding, and accentuating the theme to suit his own aesthetic purposes. His style developed as a tool for his messages, not as an end in itself. [8]

In 1920, after the failure of his first marriage, Dixon married Dorothea Lange, a portrait photographer who would gain renown for her documentary work in the Depression a decade later. Their fifteen year marriage produced two sons, Daniel Rhodes (named after Eugene Manlove Rhodes), born in 1925, and John Eaglefeather, born in 1928. Maynard Dixon entered Dorothea

Lange's life in an unusually dramatic way, perhaps expected of a primary figure of San Francisco's Bohemian community:

I told you I was in the basement most of the time, very busy working, and all these people were there a lot, many people... I'd hear them (above me) coming in the evening, and some of their footsteps I knew ... My darkroom was just below that corridor. One night there came some very peculiar sharp, clicking footsteps, and I wondered who that was. A couple of nights later I heard the same footsteps. I asked somebody, 'Who is that I heard with those sharp heels?'

'Oh, that's Maynard Dixon. Haven't you met him?'

"No, I don't know him." Well, I did meet him up there a few evenings later and six or eight months later we were married... He wore cowboy boots, that was it, with very high heels, Texas boots. [9]

People who knew Dixon at this time described him as tall, angular, thin-faced with blue eyes, long, slim particularly facile hands, and a way of looking through people. The Dixon and Lange circle in the 1920s and early 1930s included Imogen Cunningham, Ansel Adams, Roi Partridge, George Sterling, Ralph Stackpole, Gottardo Piazzoni, Lucien Labaudt, Albert Bender, Fremont Older, Paul and Winona Tomanoczy, and many other artists and writers. Dixon's studio at 728 Montgomery was full of material culture he used in his work—saddles, ropes, Pueblo pottery, Navajo rugs, and Western illustrations. This was a block of studios of artists and writers—a center of San Francisco's vibrant and colorful Bohemian life.

Dixon's work in the 1920s featured such lyrical, allegorical compositions as *Pony Boy (page 18)*, *The Wise Men (page 15)*, *The Ancients (page 19)*, *Mystery Stone (page 22)*, *Circle of Shimaikuli (page 26)*, and bold, starkly dramatic landscapes like *Cloud World (page 27)*, and *The Golden Range*. In an essay Dixon titled *Watch Your Step*, he declared:

What is the irreduceable (sic) minimum of plain common sense needed in any work, art or otherwise, to keep it from being nonsense?

Long ago (1918-19) when "modern art," (neo-impressionism, cubism, etc.) was getting under way in the U.S. I had to make a decision. I tried some experiments in non-objective painting, pure expression and whatnot, and then took a turn in the desert to think it over. I came back with the following conclusions; though subsequent work and observation have given me some serious second thoughts I have not seen the need to radically amend them.

The Circle of Shimaikuli
1922

Oil, 40″ x 36″

Private Collection

Cloud World
1925

Oil, 34" x 62"

Collection of Mr. and Mrs. Clay Lockett

The artist does not start out to manufacture "art," he tries to tell something seen, sensed or imagined — to state some kind of truth.

In this sense art is a language.

It should therefore be intelligible. It should have a core of common understanding.

The medium and form in which it is cast should be chosen with regard to the thought of feelings to be expressed.

(And here's where a lot of the fashionable and "arty" artists go wrong). The manipulation of that medium should be such as to make it an organic part of the expression, not a thing in and for itself. (The old art-for-art's-sake was that and therefore mostly sterile.)

Well, Shakespeare was right: "To thine own self be true... thou canst not then be false to any man." If the artist's own observation and experience are less important to him than an urge to be "modern" and to be always in the mode, then he has damned little self to express. At best he walks a thin and perilous line between being a genius and a horse's ass. The difference between art and arty is just about the same as the difference between smart and smarty. [10]

Dixon's mural commissions were numerous during the 1920s and 1930s. He developed panels on the S.S. *Sierra* and the S.S. *Silver State* (1921-1923), a frieze in the Room of the Dons of the Mark Hopkins Hotel (1926), a panel in the Oakland Theater (1927), a mural in the main reading room of the California State Library (1928), the dramatic *Legend of the Earth and Sun* for the Arizona Biltmore Hotel (1929), and murals for the John C. Fremont High School, Los Angeles (1933) and the Kit Carson Cafe, San Francisco (1936). Dixon's murals are structurally composed and well adapted to their architectural schemes; they always have a true mural style. The artist often adapted and included design ideas from Native American art. Most important, these works have strong silhouettes and an insistence upon composition by mass—invaluable components of mural decoration.

Throughout the 1920s, Dixon made lengthy trips into the Nevada and Arizona deserts. He went to Arizona in 1922, 1923, and 1929, and to Nevada in 1927, where he traveled for four months across the northern part of the state, through sheep country, over wild horse ranges, and into the Black Rock Desert. He and Dorothea Lange accompanied Anita Baldwin to the Hopi and Navajo country in 1923, where Dixon stayed behind for four months, finally returning home with over thirty canvases and numerous drawings.

Dixon's trips into the desert were a means of spiritual and artistic regeneration. "Otherness" and "remoteness" are basic to the idea of the West. Dixon often crossed the boundary between what was known and what is sufficiently distant to be imagined. Much of the charisma of the West, according to Joshua Taylor, has been bound up in the concept of a region which was qualitatively, not just quantitatively, different. [11] It was not simply a matter of Dixon going to the desert for artistic stimulation—he had to go for very personal and philosophic reasons. "You can't argue with the mountains," he would say, "the West is spiritually important to Americans."

During the Depression years of the 1930s, Dixon's work included a new direction toward social themes. Shaken by his observation on the dislocation of American culture during the Depression, Dixon did a series of powerful paintings depicting hobos, migrant farm workers, and city-dwellers uprooted by a pressure of Depression-era economics. This led, among other things, to a shift from an exclusively Western point of view to a more broad American outlook. Paintings such as *Destination Unknown, Free Speech, Law and Disorder,* and *Scab* are representative of his somber Depression-era works; they are now viewed as works of art comparable with John Steinbeck's *Grapes of Wrath.* While deeply concerned by the Depression, Dixon also welcomed its coming:

I like the Depression principally because it brings us back to a realization that integrity is the one thing on which social life can be built. I have tried to paint on that basis. [12]

After visiting some migrant labor camps populated by refugees from the Dust Bowl of the late 1930s, an angry Dixon wrote a letter in rebuttal to an editorial in the San Francisco *Examiner* declaring:

Their case seems hopeless, yet in their hearts they are not defeated. After a day in the carrots and peas, they still have the spirit to get out the cracked fiddle or battered guitar and play for you— the Arkansas Traveler, Oh Susanna, Casey Jones— the old backwoods tunes that mean America.

And what kind of people are they? The same kind that carried the long rifle over the Alleghanies and down the Ohio, across the Mississippi and the Plains to the Rocky Mountains; the same kind as Sam Houston and Davie Crockett, Kit Carson, Jim Bridger and California Joe. Most of them come from Missouri, Arkansas, Oklahoma and West Texas— small farmers, share croppers, farm laborers— driven out of drought, tractor farming, and foreclosure. They have sold their last few holdings, tools, hogs, mules, at pawn shop prices to cross 1500 miles of semi-desert to reach the promised land of sunshine and plenty that our boosters have been advertising for fifty years— golden California— and so they find it— golden for those who have gold. [13]

Allegory
1933-35

Oil, 40″ x 36″

Collection of Daniel R. Dixon

The Plains
1931-33

Oil, 25″ x 30″

Dr. Harold R. Clark Memorial Collection
Brigham Young University

Mural and easel painting dominated Dixon's work throughout the rest of the 1930s and early 1940s. He painted murals for the post offices in Martinez and Canoga Park, *The Arrival of Fremont in California* for the John C. Fremont High School in Los Angeles (1933), and Indian panels, *The Indian Yesterday* and *The Indian Today,* for the entrance to the Bureau of Indian Affairs in the Department of the Interior in Washington, D.C. Studio compositions during this period included such visionary and imaginative works as *Shapes of Fear, Allegory (page 30), Men of the Red Earth (page 39), Home of the Blackfeet (page 67), Deer Heaven, Merging of Spring and Winter,* and one of Dixon's important works *Earth Knower,* painted during 1931-32.

The first several years of the Depression were a trial for artists and Dixon found himself in a "bleak time, work and worry, prospects dark." Dixon painted over a hundred easel pictures, many oil sketches and drawings and only sold two dozen of them. What meager sales there were, such as the purchase of *Shapes of Fear* by the Henry W. Ranger Fund, kept the Dixon family safe for a while. In 1931, Maynard and Dorothea decided to go to Taos, New Mexico, and accompanied by sons Daniel and John, spent six months in an old adobe house, without electricity, water, or plumbing. Dixon painted works such as *Yonder the Navajos, Como Se Pasa la Vida (page 34), Watchers from the Housetops (page 35), Antonio Mirabal (page 2), and Campo Santo.* He studied cloud formations for a series of paintings, *Skies of New Mexico,* and renewed acquaintance with Frank Hoffman, Ernest Blumenschein (whom he had met during his New York days), and Mabel Dodge Luhan, and visited the "grand old lady of American letters," Mary Austin, at Santa Fe.

The family left San Francisco again in the summer of 1933 and traveled to Southern Utah, visiting the quiet Mormon towns and camping in Zion National Park which provided scenes described by Dixon as "not as beautiful as Canyon de Chelly but grander—a new world to us— magnificent and awesome by moonlight." Finished canvases such as *Great White Throne, High in the Morning, Fields of Tocquerville,* and *Approach to Zion* celebrate Dixon's rhythmical and harmonious compositions, as well as the form and colors in his paintings.

By 1935, the marriage of Maynard Dixon and Dorothea Lange was ending. Dixon was sixty then, increasingly incapacitated by emphysema, and despite his love for his family, disciplined work habits and powerful will, he would write, "tragic interlude: divorce." In 1937, Dixon married Edith Hamlin, an established San Francisco artist and muralist. Strong-willed and talented, she shared many of his interests. Drawn by his colorful, radiant paintings and his keen, agile humor, Edith and Maynard became friends, caring for, encouraging, and helping each other in her Telegraph Hill home and his Montgomery Street studio.

That year also brought an inquiry from Yale University's Institute of Human Relations on the possibility of Dixon doing illustrations for a book on social and economic inequalities. Dixon responded characteristically:

Your letter is very interesting and it stirs contradictory impulses. One is to laugh, one is to weep, and the other is to write you a high, wide and handsome American razz.

Having spent nearly twenty years as an illustrator of books and magazines and six years as a designer of advertising, in addition to having been a painter of the life of the West for twenty-five years, all of which brought me into contact with many kinds of people, brown, yellow and white, you may see that, in my own way, I have also studied the activities of human beings. Therefore, my conclusion is that the only people who might benefit by the kind of books you propose to issue are those who steadfastly refuse to acknowledge the facts you seek to present. If you do not realize by this time that people are already well aware of the tragic inequalities of life under the present set-up and that what they want is not a reiteration of the facts but some definite way to remedy those inequalities, then I should say for scientists such as you, the case is hopeless.

You make me think of the bozo who tried to down a jolt of whiskey without letting it touch his tonsils. What most of you profs need is a little more corral dust in your flapjacks. [14]

In 1939, Dixon and Edith Hamlin moved to Tucson, Arizona, where he hoped the climate would relieve a life-long respiratory ailment. In leaving San Francisco he felt he had not yet completed an original ambition to interpret the West for the rest of the world:

I've done all right as far as I've gone, but I'm not done yet. People need more than ever some realization of this country's pioneer strength — some of its stark simplicity. It's got to carry us through this evil period. [15]

Maynard and Edith lived in Tucson during the winter and spent the summers in a studio-home at Mt. Carmel, Utah, near the rich colors of Zion National Park. He continued to paint works that captured the sense of silence and space, bleakness and beauty.

The last six years of Dixon's life brought wide public recognition and appreciation for his work — an eagerness to explore new expressions and a gallant but losing fight for his health. Friends and colleagues were deeply impressed with the humor, good company, and youthful spirit of the semi-invalid — with his continued determination to work as an artist. In 1942, Dixon illustrated his last book, the Limited Edition Club's new publication of Francis Parkman's *Oregon Trail*. The assignment was close to his life-long interest and talents, and this classic account of Parkman's adventures among the Plains Indians and frontiersmen resulted in an acclaimed set of drawings and color plates.

Near the end of Dixon's productive career as an illustrator, artist, and muralist, fellow artist Millard Sheets arranged a retrospective exhibition at Scripps College in 1945. At the opening,

Como Se Pasa la Vida
1931-32

Oil, 25″ x 30″

Collection of Helen Dixon

Watchers from the Housetops
1931-32

Oil, 30" x 25"

Collection of the Phoenix Art Museum,
Western Art Associates Purchase

which Dixon was too ill to attend, Millard Sheets relayed his greetings and a message from the artist—pure Dixon in its pungent individuality:

But long ago—about 1915, when "modern art" first hit the U. S. A. — I had to make a hard decision. Should I go along with the "new movement", adopt a novel and fashionable point of view, get my ideas "imported", — or should I look at my world with more candid eyes, be plainly honest with myself and so achieve something perhaps not startling but at least sincere.

As often before, I went again into the desert to find an answer—and it was not far to seek. Well, there is the empty desert; there are arid mountains; the shimmer in the ashen heat of noon, a reality that appears unreal, challenging the imagination. And there is the Indian who can withdraw into himself and be as silent and unresponsive as a stone. You cannot argue with silence. It returns your question to you, to your own inner silence which becomes aware—a mystical something that is neither reason nor intelligence nor intuition, a recognition of some nameless truth that may not be denied. So my choice was made; I must find in this visible world the forms, the colors, the relationships that for me are the most true of it, and find a way to state them clearly so that the painting may pass on something of my vision.

But don't think it was all as dreamy as that. Here I was in the midst of the Real Thing—my western world — and my mind was set to tell the truth of it on paper and on canvas, and that meant work. It meant constant observation and constant drawing.

But to get rid of the short-cut habits of my illustration days, to emerge from the ways of quick composition and the monotony of black-and-white into thoughtful planning and true color was not so easy. All this time I was turning out paintings (of a sort) — my vision and my point of view gradually changing. While I did not tie to any of the current 'isms' of modern art, neither did I shun them. They were part of our times. Some painters have accused me of a narrow localism in my work — of refusing to learn from modern art (now 30 years old) — but little they know how often I have seen some painting of mine hung next to one of the newer school where the contrast sent me to my lair in shame and vowing repentence. From these things, from my own two eyes and the desert silence I learned. So finally I came to the point where the illustrators said I was a pretty good painter, the painters said I was a pretty good writer, and the writers said I was a pretty good illustrator. [16]

In 1945, Dixon's final year, the Santa Fe Railway commissioned him to do a mural design of the Grand Canyon for its new city ticket office in Los Angeles. Although it was seemingly beyond his declining energies, he designed the mural, assisted by his wife Edith Hamlin, and artists Buck Weaver and Ray Strong. By this time, Dixon needed oxygen even to struggle from his bed; he was moved by wheelchair to the mural in an outdoor ramada.

The final days are poignantly remembered by Edith Hamlin:

With the 'Old Master' increasingly confined to his home base, the Dixon casa became a rendezvous, even a sort of pilgrimage. Around the invalid-artist, lounging in characteristic long blue Chinese coolie-coat and Indian moccasins on the sunlit Tucson veranda, gathered those who loved the man, his keen talk and agile humor, and the easy hospitality of his home. To have been with the lean, bearded sage (with a mischievous eye) is a cherished memory to those who shared that time. He was one of those rich personalities who leaves his clear imprint upon others. His work, reaching many more over the years, expresses the man more truly than any words. There, plainly visible in forthright, basic design and color, dynamic composition and masterly drawing, lies the unmistakable signature of Maynard Dixon. [17]

Maynard Dixon died November 14, 1946, in Tucson, Arizona, remembered and recognized as an interpreter of the American West with visions and images entirely his own. His ashes were placed beneath a bronze plaque on a ridge overlooking his studio in Mt. Carmel. One of his autobiographical poems, *The Years* (c. 1935), conveys an epithaph:

Now as the years pass more quickly,
and I become better acquainted
with the slowly approaching visage of death—
seeing more often old friends and relations depart
beyond the reach of my understanding;
now that no longer I feel the white fire
of youthful ambition, nor the blind impetuous urge
of young passion;
and the great illusion has faded, only to linger
a high and immortal dream— yet I am content.
Ever more do I see that out of the turmoil comes order;
ever more do I know that to win some happiness here
I must hold myself up, above petty disputes and distinctions,
keeping some largeness of heart
alike for those who trust me and for those who distrust me;
to share with them my long held vision of Beauty.
Yes, this is enough. So unhurriedly I will pass
peacefully, yes, content, under the desert stars. [18]

Footnotes

1. Peter H. Hassrick. *The Way West: Art of Frontier America.* New York, 1977.

2. Grant Wallace. *Maynard Dixon: Painter and Poet of the Far West.* San Francisco Art Research Project, W.P.A., 1937.

3. Maynard Dixon. "Arizona in 1900." *Arizona Highways,* February, 1942.

4. Ibid.

5. Maynard Dixon. "Navajo Land." *Arizona Highways,* May, 1942.

6. *Rim-Rock and Sage: The Collected Poems of Maynard Dixon.* San Francisco, 1977.

7. Maynard Dixon. "An American Rhythm." Unpublished letter in the collection of Edith Hamlin. (1925).

8. Donald J. Hagerty, Editor and Interviewer. *Edith Hamlin: A California Artist.* (Oral history) American Studies Program, University of California, Davis, 1981.

9. Oakland Museum. *Celebrating a Collection—the Work of Dorothea Lange.* Oakland, 1978.

10. Maynard Dixon. "Watch Your Step." Unpublished essay in the Maynard Dixon Collection, Bancroft Library, University of California, Berkeley (c. 1930).

11. Joshua Taylor. *America as Art.* Washington, D.C. Smithsonian Institution Press, 1976.

12. *Los Angeles Times,* April 9, 1933.

13. Maynard Dixon. "Who are the Dust Bowlers?" *San Francisco Examiner,* March 29, 1939.

14. Maynard Dixon. Unpublished letter in the collection of Edith Hamlin. (April 17, 1937).

15. *San Francisco Examiner.* October 3, 1939.

16. Maynard Dixon. Unpublished letter in the Maynard Dixon Collection, Bancroft Library, University of California, Berkeley (1945).

17. Edith Hamlin. "Maynard Dixon—the Later Years." Unpublished manuscript (1950).

18. *Rim-Rock and Sage: The Collected Poems of Maynard Dixon.* San Francisco, 1977.

Men of the Red Earth
1931-32

Oil, 36″ x 40″

Courtesy of the Student Body
Gardena High School
Gardena, California

The Native American Portrayed
Donald J. Hagerty

While the precise cultural and economic significance of the frontier in American life still remains a matter of controversy, there is little doubt that the role of the West and the Native American in the American imagination is enormous. When we enter the realm of image, popularized through works of art and literature about the West or through the patterns that are reflected in American speech and attitude, it becomes quite clear that certain aspects of the frontier—the cowboy, settler, gold miner, and particularly the Native American—have been, and remain today, important themes in our culture.

From an artistic point of view, one of the most important and vital images of the West was that of a place where one might escape from the artificial and corrupting boundaries of society into an open and spontaneous relationship with nature. This view of the West as an escape has usually included an important and sympathetic role for the Native American.[1]

By the time Frederick Jackson Turner delivered his paper, *The Significance of the Frontier in American History*, in 1893 (the year Dixon became a professional artist), Americans already knew the frontier had been an important part of their culture. A number of individuals in different artistic fields had made an indelible mark by giving literary, dramatic, and artistic structure to the image of the Old West. Among them were the showman William F. Cody (Buffalo Bill), novelist Owen Wister, and artists Frederic Remington and Charles M. Russell. Remington and Russell, along with many other artists, became summarizing masters and purveyors of the Western scene. Their method was to respond to the cultural need for an image of the West as a place of epic action, heroic individualism, and liberated wildness, creating the images which would come to stand for a vision of the American West as a special landscape in the imagination.

Artists are individuals whose talents for expression in a variety of media lead them to take on the vital function of conveying visually the images and patterns that represent our culture. There is, however, a special kind of artist who sets traditions into creative tension with his own vision of the world. Such an artist's work has a significant impact because we recognize in it depth and complexity that transcends more limited interpretations. Artistic images of the West have been the product of a complex interplay between cultural patterns, popular artistic presentations based upon these patterns, and the work of unique artists who somehow found the ability to link a fresh encounter with experience in the West to their own culture.[2] One of these artists was Maynard Dixon.

Dixon's interest in and sympathetic vision toward the Native American were formed early in his life. An early (1887) pack trip with his father into the remote wilderness of the Kern River Canyon and Kaweah Range in the Sierra east of Fresno provided views of the dwindling remnants of the Mono Indians. Their lonely silhouettes against the long horizon were lasting impressions. A few sketches survive from this period, and already there was anticipation of a more direct and forceful manner in his work. Dixon's early illustration period (1893-1899) as an artist for the *Overland Monthly, Land of Sunshine,* and the San Francisco *Morning Call* gave him additional opportunities in the development of illustration techniques. Field trips to Wintun and Maidu *rancherias* provided exposure to the rapidly disappearing culture of the California Indian.

Renowned Indian authority and "booster" of the Southwest, Charles F. Lummis offered encouragement for Dixon's work and critical assessment. In an article in the *Land of Sunshine* he observed:

Mr. Dixon's largest talent has to do with humanity and the horse. He paints and draws good landscapes, but is at his strongest in type and drawing action. He has an unusual "feeling" for the ethnological truth. There are so many who can show us, most artistically, how they think an Indian . . . or any other picturesque type ought to look; so few who seem able to portray him as he does look. And when one pretends to represent a racial type, the first duty of art is truthfulness. The second is to translate the face into terms of grace, without losing the typical character. The work of any man who can really draw types and not lose them has a serious value beyond, and possibly above, its mere pictorial worth. An artist so young and already so distinctive will "bear watching." [3]

Between 1900 and 1946, Dixon made frequent trips to Arizona, New Mexico, Oregon, Montana, Nevada, Utah, and Idaho observing and depicting the transitional cultures of Mojave, Pima, Bannock, Shoshone, Maricopa, Apache, Paiute, Navajo, Blackfoot, Hopi, Pueblo, Yaqui, Papago, and other Indian groups. He was artist, poet, historian, folklorist, ethnologist, and cultural anthropologist, with an eye for details and technical skill to record his perceptions.

His first trip to the Southwest in 1900 produced a notable series of pencil and wash portrait studies of Mojave Indians around Fort Mojave and Roberts Ranch along the Colorado River near Needles. Powerful and sensitive, they are striking ethnographic and documentary images of solemn silent individuals, forced to live in a rapidly changing, alien world, yet determined to retain their tribal identity and image. Dixon returned to the Southwest in 1902, traveling among the Hopi and Navajo in Northern Arizona. Leaving Winslow by wagon, he headed toward the Hopi country, sketching around Oraibi, down Oraibi Wash to Polacca and Walpi and on to Ganado, sixty five miles from the railroad, making endless drawings of the Navajo around Lorenzo Hubbell's trading post. Existing Dixon sketches show Navajo at Chinlee, landscape views of the broken country along Chinlee Creek, Keams Canyon, and the magnificent grandeur of Canyon de Chelly.

When sketching Dixon used anything that could be drawn upon—scrap paper, sketch paper, wrapping paper, backs of bills, announcements, and cards. Dixon was intuitively perceptive and

The Ancient
1915

Oil, 20″ x 12″

Collection of Katherine H. Haley

The Trail to Pei-ki-hat-tsoh
1912

Oil, 20″ x 30″

Collection of Earl C. Adams

was capable of determining the inner feelings of individuals he was sketching. His field studies are usually annotated with year, location, and occasionally other information such as color. Dixon used ink, pencil, charcoal, or crayon to get information down for future use; and he got it down quickly, directly, and truthfully. He produced literally thousands of these drawings in his lifetime, storing images and memories which would be used in many later works. His proficiency and robust draughtsmanship, in a variety of media, formed the foundation for his images of the Native American. Among all the Native Americans he drew or painted, Dixon would especially remember the Navajo—his singing Indians:

As they rode across the long valleys or through echoing canyons their high-keyed lilting songs could be heard from far off through the clean high air. With their sheep and goats and ponies, their little cornfields and shelters of juniper boughs; their igloo-like hogans; their painted moccasins and painted dancers; eagle feathers, turquoise and glinting silver in the firelight, the shrill high chant and rattles; sweating bodies in the sharp November night. And there, the voices of eagles, coyotes, bears— but wilder, fiercer— were my Indian ghosts again. [4]

Dixon's respect and appreciation for the Native American was a part of his deep reverence for the Western landscape. He would come to consider the Native American an elemental phenomenon, like rain on the hills or clouds in the skies. Dixon felt the Indian was nearer to these natural elements than he was. The Indian to Dixon, as to many others before him, was a symbol of "natural man," and as such stood between him and nature and acted as an interpreter of those forces which he so admired. By 1905, Dixon was painting such works as *Navajo Women, Navajo Girls Bathing, Old Apache, In Navajo Land, Moqui Town Crier,* and *Bannock Girl.* Since many of these have disappeared, we can only speculate about their effect upon existing work of the same period. Probably small, averaging about 8 x 10 inches, they would undoubtedly forecast Dixon's understanding of color and suggestion of mood.

Dixon's next visit to the West was during his New York illustration period. At the invitation of Charles Stuart Moody, an old frontiersman from Idaho, Dixon in 1909 went to Northern Idaho— after the arid Southwest, a country alien to him in its cool waters and dense forests. He visited old-timers in their log cabins, stayed with the Nez Perce around Lake Pend Oreille and with Kootenay and Flathead Indians in their tepees in the Flathead Valley and at St. Ignatius Mission. Impressionist-like paintings such as *Flathead Indian and Pony, Flathead Tepees, Corrals of St. Ignatius,* and *Home of the Halfbreed* convey Dixon's increasing proficiency of color and mood. There is less emphasis on ethnographic accuracy in the subject and more on the presentation of the subject matter.

The four mural panels painted by Dixon in 1912 for the home of Anita Baldwin McClaughry at Sierra Madre near Pasadena signal a change from the literal, realistic portrayal of the Native

American to a more poetic and mystical interpretation. The murals *Victory Song, Envoys of Peace,* *(pages 10, 11), The Pool,* and *The Ghost Eagle* project a dramatic narrative of the vanished life of the Plains Indian.

I do not paint Indians . . . merely because they are picturesque objects, but because through them I can express that phantasy (sic) of freedom and space and thought, which will give the world a sentiment about these people which is inspiring and uplifting.

In these panels I wished especially to interpret the old life of the Indian who inhabited the prairie lands of northern Montana, Dakota or Wyoming fifty years ago to bring out the poetic, rather than the harsh, brutal part of their lives. [5]

One of his models was George Whitewing, a Winnebago who became a close friend and influential advisor on Native American culture and would pose for many of Dixon's studio compositions.

Accompanied by his wife and five-year-old daughter Constance, Dixon spent several months of 1915 in Arizona, sketching and painting around San Carlos and Fort Apache, and on up to the Grand Canyon. Numerous paintings were completed such as *Apache Camp, The Navajo, The Scouts, Apache Acorn Gathers (page 78),* and the visionary *What an Indian Thinks (page 46).*

The summer of 1917 brought a commission from Louis W. Hill, President of the Great Northern Railroad, for a group of paintings featuring Glacier National Park and the Blackfoot Indians. Accompanied by his daughter Constance and noted illustrator Frank Hoffman, he spent August, September, and October painting, visiting Charles M. Russell at Lake McDermott, and camping with the Blackfoot on Cutbank Creek. Six families of Blackfoot, led by Two Guns White Calf, sang, told stories and legends, and served as models. Maynard and Constance attended the initiation of new members into the Brave Dog Society (Blackfoot Police) and were the only non-Indian guests at a private ceremony. The results of this trip were paintings such as *Blackfeet Historians, The Grandmother, Picture Writing, Blackfeet Camp,* and many drawings.

In the 1920s, Dixon's paintings and murals took on a new searching, intepretive focus. Disturbed by his observation of the Indian cultures in transition and of the disappearance of the Old West, he began to seek a projection of that increasingly rare place, where the Native American stood in almost mystical relation with the outer world, close to the earth, as much a part of the landscape as the mesas and canyons. Already a master draughtsman, Dixon in the 1920s was becoming a virtuoso colorist. His deliberately simplified palette showed strength in new color values, often pitched to the luminosity of the desert country and the earth tones in Native American art. Studio works such as *Medicine Woman (page 14), Pony Boy (page 18), Mystery Stone (page 22), Ledges of*

What An Indian Thinks
1915

Oil, 40″ x 50″

Private Collection

End House of Walpi
1923

Oil, 25″ x 30″

Private Collection

Sunland (page 57), and *The Ancients (page 19)*, express rhythm and balance in composition, color, and decorative value. There is a sense of space, simplicity of theme and yet dynamic organization and silent poetry in these compositions. The visual presentations of silence and space were influenced by Dixon's knowledge of Native American culture:

The Indian is enigmatic and so he fascinates us, he does away with the superficialities and comes straight to the point. But the most peculiar and subtle thing about him is his faculty of using silence as a means of communication.[6]

Dixon, sometimes accompanied by his wife, photographer Dorothea Lange, continued his trips into the Southwest. In 1922, they visited the Navajo reservation in Arizona around Kayenta and Tuba City. Guided by John and Ned Wetherill, discoverers of some of the most spectacular cliff dwellings found yet in the Southwest, Dixon made studies around Red Lake, Monument Valley, Black Mesa, and Betatakin. Again in 1923, as the guests of Anita Baldwin, he and Dorothea returned to the Hopi and Navajo country. After the women left for home, Dixon remained for four months at Tavapochamo and Walpi, making friends with one of the Snake Priests, wandering around the villages studying traditions and ceremonies, and observing the beginning of the winter cycle of Kachina dances. He described this extended stay as giving him "a sense of being part of nature, of timelessness of existence, a closeness to the inner reality of life." Many of Dixon's notable works come from this period: *The Wise Men (page 15)*, *Circle of Shimaikuli (page 26)*, *Witch of Sikyatki* and *Study for Migration #2*. His emotional attachment to the Hopi and Navajo country is evident in a letter to Robert Macbeth, his New York art dealer:

You would suppose that here in the ancient Province of Tusayan (now Hopi Land) that I would have plenty of time for everything. But it is not our kind of time, — you can't count it. It is made only of days, moons and eternity. Then also if I have a date with a rock at a certain angle of the sun and shadow, and another with an Indian who lives 2 miles away up a steep trail and from that down to the house in time to chop wood, carry water and cook my dinner and be through in time to make a drawing afterward and then write 3 or 4 letters — then out in the morning to sketch or maybe go to the store (an Indian store) or perhaps ride 12 miles to Mishong-novi to see a ceremony, get back after dark, cook, wash up and start a canvas of what I have seen — why you can see the days are pretty well filled.

As for the country itself, and the people, they are wonderful — always wonderful! — Now is the real autumn, right on the sharp edge of winter, with the sting of frost in the long blue shadows, and a flood of pale yellow sun like an hallucination coming over the far blue rim of mesas to the south. Away out in the golden-brown flats the few cottonwood trees flame like small orange torches and the dust of a band of sheep follows it, a faint golden ghost. The thin distinct voice of an Indian singing a wild wavering song comes dropping down from the tall rocks, — the small delicate drift of blue smoke and the fine odor of cedar burning; — and above all the endless empty blue sky — the sky where there is no time.

These Hopis are remarkable people. They must have come from the south and brought their corn and their pottery and their weaving with them. Small, kindly, home people, very different from the fierce hunting tribes of the plains and mountains. There lingers something of remote antiquity about them—they feel of the stone age.

They still believe and act as our forefathers did 20,000 years ago. They are here in the midst of this age of steel and electricity a little remnant of the stone age still living!

Many people would come here and not see all this. They might see only that these Indians are poor and dirty and lousy; that the kids go naked and are unspeakably filthy; that they have little water and no sanitation; that they believe in magic and have savage customs. But when you see one of their ceremonies—there for an hour something fine flashes out clear; there is savage beauty in them, — they have imagination. They have dignity and form. These things are for the archaeologist and the painter to understand. From them the scientist recreates the ancient world; the artist creates a new one.

In these later canvases you will probably see traces of all this. There is something of magic in it, and legends endow it with strange meanings. The imagination moves free and the past and present are one. So the visions of the old days have been as important to my work as things actually seen. [7]

From his visits and his studies of Indian legends, Dixon wrote two books in 1923. *Injun Babies* was a collection of Native American children's stories he had told to his small daughter. *Poems and Seven Drawings,* published by the Grabhorn Press in San Francisco, contained twelve of his poems illustrated with dynamic pen and ink drawings. His trips into Navajo and Hopi country would also turn Dixon into a strong supporter of John Collier's Indian Defense Association's efforts to help Native Americans protect their land rights.

The early part of 1929 found Dixon working on one of his outstanding Native American murals, *The Legend of Earth and Sun,* an eight by twenty-five foot painting for the dining room of the Arizona Biltmore Hotel in Phoenix. Elements of Native American culture were used in simple yet dramatic visual presentations. The dominating figure of Father Sun lends rays of light and warmth to Mother Earth, making the corn, symbol of plenty, grow into a productive plant. The mural portrays no particular tale, but was Dixon's tale of the eternal story of Father Sun and Mother Earth, connected with Pueblo Indian legends—the bounty of nature and the promise of the gods that man will prosper. The beginning of the Depression years provided Dixon with new impressions:

Without any sense of personal failure, I had a growing feeling of oppression—of something ominous and unavoidable impending—of being caught in the slowly closing jaws of a vise, of complete helplessness in the grip of fate. [8]

Neolithic Afternoon
1930

Oil, 36″ x 40″

Private Collection

Ledges of Sunland
1922

Oil, 25" x 30"

Collection of Brigham Young University, Provo, Utah
Gift of Mr. and Mrs. Larry P. Ullman, Mr. and Mrs. Delbert
S. Hawkley and Mr. James P. Kelly.

Dixon would turn to the Native American and the land for emotional and visual responses. Always sensitive to changes in American culture, he had the feeling of being surrounded by vague, dangerous, threatening forms. Out of this feeling and a need to express it developed *Shapes of Fear,* painted in 1930—a group of four Indian-like figures, robed, their faces shrouded from view. This extraordinary composition, which won the prestigious Ranger Award in 1932, was like the arid country the figures represent: massive, ageless, with a sense of mystery and dread. Three more of Dixon's compositions, the acclaimed *Earth Knower, Allegory (page 30),* and *Men of the Red Earth (page 39),* were painted in 1931-1932 as a spiritual response to the despair of the Depression and a reminder of man's dependence and identification with the earth:

You can't argue with those desert mountains— and if you live among them enough— like the Indian does— you don't want to. They have something for us much more real than some imported art style.

I tried to express this idea in the The Earth Knower. *He is a sage, calm Indian who stands against his own background of mountains, from which he draws his health, wealth, religion and pattern of living. While we get panic-stricken over "the Market" the Indian puffs his pipe and looks at the sky. The West is big, slow, grand country, with a style all its own. We scurry around it like nervous ants and scarcely take time to let it seep into our souls.* [9]

These paintings exemplify again one of Dixon's fundamental beliefs—the interdependence and blending of basic cultural elements of the Native American with the drama of nature. There is a sense of mystical detachment and timelessness. They are permeated with a vital force springing from the contact of the artist with his subject—organic rather than consciously organized by any fashionable formula or rule. Like many of his later works, they are a combination of remembrances and representations of idea-related themes, drawn from Native American cultural traditions and his own direct participation and experience in a transitional frontier. Once asked to comment on his work, he declared: "It is a means to the end. It is my way of saying what I want you to comprehend. It is my testimony in regard to life."

Maynard Dixon devoted much of his life to depicting in drawings, paintings, and murals the West of mountains and deserts, rugged canyons—sun dominated landscapes that were the ancient home of the Native American. He had a special sympathy for the inhabitants of this immense and silent land. He was an American painter in the broadest sense. His portrayal of the Native American and the Western landscape was deeply personal and independent of prevailing fashions. It had a profound sense of area, transcending specific location to express the inner spirit and nature of America. Dixon was that rare kind of artist—a man at peace with himself, who had an intuitive vision of the West and its Native American inhabitants.

Footnotes

1. Joshua Taylor. *America as Art.* Washington, D.C.,
   Smithsonian Institution Press, 1976.

2. Ibid.

3. Charles F. Lummis. "A California Illustrator—L. Maynard
   Dixon and his Work." *Land of Sunshine,* December, 1898.

4. Maynard Dixon. "Arizona in 1900." *Arizona Highways,*
   February, 1942.

5. Los Angeles *Times,* August 2, 1913.

6. *Daily Californian,* December 4, 1925.

7. Maynard Dixon. Unpublished letter (1923) in the
   collection of Edith Hamlin.

8. Grant Wallace. *Maynard Dixon: Painter and Poet of the Far
   West.* San Francisco Art Research Project, W.P.A., 1937.

9. Los Angeles *Times,* April 9, 1933.

Philosopher
1931

Oil, 20″ x 16″

Private Collection

Christmas Eve Procession
1931

Oil, 16" x 20"

Dr. Harold R. Clark Memorial Collection
Brigham Young University

Maynard Dixon: An Artist, A Friend
Ansel Adams

Maynard Dixon once paid me what I considered an extraordinary compliment, indeed, an honor: he told me that he liked my work because he felt that I knew what I was doing, that I was a good craftsman. Such a compliment meant all the more to me coming as it did from a man who was a great friend and a fine artist, a man who approached life, as well as art, with courage, conviction, and strength, a man whom I greatly admired.

There are those, and they do annoy me, who would dismiss Dixon as a "scenery" or "poster" painter. Dixon did his share of potboilers, as have we all, but he also created a number of works that were magnificently inspired, that will long endure, and that firmly establish Maynard Dixon as a true artist of the American West.

Dixon stands as part of an American artistic tradition—an almost pantheistic devotion to the grandeur of the the natural scene—yet he stands apart from that tradition as well, for his was a vision that rejected sentimentality and romanticization, in favor of realism and understanding.

Dixon belonged to and in the West. Born in Fresno in 1875, and venturing for the first time into the Southwest in 1900, Dixon reveled in the beauty and the freedom that abounded in the West, and he spent much of his life resisting the steady inroads made on both in the name of civilization.

The kind of artist that we then had in the West was different from those in the East. Denied the ready audience (or the patrons) enjoyed by the Eastern artist, those in the West frequently found it necessary to devote time and energy to journalism or advertising to make a living. Economic necessity forced Dixon to pursue a dual career in professional art and "real" art, and took him in 1907 to New York for a five year sojourn fighting the constant deadlines faced by a commercial artist and illustrating publications not on the basis of his perceptions of the West but to meet Eastern misconceptions.

Dixon returned to the West in 1912, his ideal confirmed: neither the West nor his vision of it could conform to the romanticized, histrionic, hopelessly exaggerated view popularized by most Eastern and some Western artists. He also returned with a more developed sense of abstraction, favorably influenced, I suspect, by Impressionist art he had seen in New York. His approach to art had advanced far beyond the Frederic Remington-inspired drawings of his youth. The most productive period of his life followed.

It was during the early 1920s that I first met Maynard Dixon, and we became great friends during the 1930s. Dixon would frequently visit us, or we him. When we were together—in San Francisco, Berkeley, Yosemite, or, in his later years, in Utah, or Arizona—Dixon would never converse much. He did not need to. He was one of those rare and wonderful companions who did not carry with

Maynard Dixon 1943
by Ansel Adams

them a requirement that one engage in constant conversation. We had our occasional discussions of matters quite profound, but for the most part while visiting he would draw or read. The wonderfully warm feeling he radiated—a feeling of recognition, of support, of universal compassion, and of dedication to his art—rendered verbalization unnecessary, even superfluous.

Which is not to say that Dixon was a less than engaging conversationalist. He possessed what I would call a creative cynicism. He had a talent for characterizing people in terse, perceptive, very cynical, but never really unkind statements. I remember his turning this particular talent on the hero of his youth, Frederic Remington, a man whom he judged to be "one of the few who really understood horses." That was Dixon's way of saying that Remington, a significant artist in his own right, knew a great deal about the West, knew the cowpunchers and the corrals, and the horses, of course, but did not really comprehend the major concept—the important concept—that of the land, of the West itself.

Dixon, on the other hand, grasped the entirety and the enormousness of that concept. He, like few I have known, appreciated the whole of the land, as well as its parts and their interrelationships. For him, the West was uncrowded, unlittered, unorganized, and above all, vital and free. The horizons were sufficiently distant to inspire dreams and desires, and provided more than enough space to promise fulfillment. Mere possession of the land could produce results that ranged from inconsequential to harmful, while the eye itself could encompass fantastic phenomena of plain, mountain, mesa, and sky.

Dixon also held sacred the primitive simplicity of the American Indians who lived and moved amidst the grandeur of the West. Their way of life and art was in close harmony with the primal realities—the sun, sky, earth, and space. Dixon, who made numerous lengthy trips into the Southwest, gained an impressive—and more importantly—a true understanding of the Indians of the region. He resisted and rejected such popular characterizations as that of the "Noble Red Man." Rather, he understood that the Indian philosophy and way of life—and Indian art and design as well—were more intense, more aware, and better than most observers could comprehend. Dixon realized that the Indian was not in combat with his environment, as harsh and inhospitable as it might seem to the outsider, but rather lived in tune with and as part of that environment.

One of my favorite Dixon paintings, *Earth Knower*, epitomizes his feeling for the desert Southwest and its native population. At once that painting communicates the grandeur, the expanse, the majesty of the Southwest, the arid sparseness of the region, and the serenity of an Indian who truly knows—indeed, is part of—the land. The achievement of *Earth Knower* is perfected by the unity of style and color and design with which Dixon imbued the painting.

Mes-i-ké-ber
1900

Pencil, 11″ x 8″

Collection of Edith Hamlin

Two Eagles
1932

Oil, 30" x 40"

Collection of Senator and Mrs. Barry Goldwater

In the paintings, drawings, and sketches of Maynard Dixon, one finds no indication of a self-conscious effort to record his times. He gloried in his Western roots, sparking occasional charges of pretentiousness with his black Stetson, his Stevensonian moustache, his cowboy boots, and his priceless Navajo silver belt. He knew how to use a six-shooter, and taught our son—Skeeter, as he called Michael—how to wield that legendary weapon of the West against fence-straddling tin cans. He was a genuine product of the West; there was nothing about him that did not belong in the West or that was less than genuine.

During the Depression, Dixon did shift the principal focus of his art to the breadlines, the docks, the picket lines of the period, because, as he once told me, his then wife, the photographer Dorothea Lange, prevailed upon him to subjugate his art to the demands of politics and social criticism. He did a considerable amount of painting of this type, little, however, that was noteworthy. He explored the art of "social significance," as some called it, found that his was a different world, and returned to his beloved desert. As he himself explained it, he felt that he was doing more for the world by painting that in which he believed, that which could be called beauty or expression. He returned to the great human and natural realities as he—and he alone—saw and felt them. His brief absence from his own world had served to reinforce and reaffirm his place in it.

Though Dixon may have temporarily focused his art on the social themes of the 1930s, he never forced his art to fit the preconceived rules of whatever school of art or movement was momentarily "in." He had, in fact, a healthy and instinctive distrust for the world of organized art. He was particularly critical of the San Francisco Art Institute where there was repeatedly exhibited a tendency on the part of students and faculty to imitate the style of whatever artist was serving as "artist in residence." I also remember his reaction to the painting of a French-influenced artist at the Ahwahnee Hotel in Yosemite. While I found the artist's use of Indian basket designs in a highly stylized, contemporary wall decoration highly striking, Dixon reacted as if in horror to what he viewed as the debasement of one art form in the name of another, and certainly less authentic, one.

Dixon never conformed his art to the rules or demands of any school or "ism." He knew that he was a fine artist, and, unlike many another practitioner of the plastic arts whom I have known, he simply did not care whether the viewer liked his work or not. He brought to his work a strength, a total feeling of security, a love that was highly rational and completely well-founded.

Dixon's personal life caused him considerable anguish. He reached a nadir in the mid-1930s when his second wife, Dorothea Lange, a social activist who truly felt that she had a destiny, found greater philosophical compatibility and personal intensity with another man. Fortunately for Dixon, he himself was able to develop a relationship of a similar intensity with the artist Edith Hamlin, who was really a godsend for him. Edith kept the spark going for the years that were left to Dixon.

Dixon abandoned San Francisco, his home for more than four decades, in 1937. He had grown tired of the politics of art and the life of a city, and he along with Edith sought and found succor in Arizona and Utah.

I saw him less than a year before his death in 1946. He knew that life was ebbing away from him, and he apologized for not being as lively as he had been. But he also stated emphatically that he desired, that he longed to do more work before the end.

His desire to continue to create—to see, to sketch, to paint, to reveal—served Dixon well. For him, art was not a way of life; it was life.

Juan Chino
1900

Pencil and Chalk, 13″ x 7½″

Collection of Edith Hamlin

Round Dance
1931

Oil, 16″ x 20″

Dr. Harold R. Clark Memorial Collection
Brigham Young University

Montana, 1917
Constance Dixon

What American city-child like myself has not dreamed of living with the Indians? For me it came true in 1917 when my father took me with him on his trip to Montana.

We lived with the Blackfoot for perhaps a month or more at their camp on Cutbank Creek. While my father painted, I played with the Indian kids. We were expected to do some chores around camp, and I remember riding an old swaybacked pony, with two other kids, to go up the creek and gather fallen cottonwood boughs for the fires. We had no saddle, not even a blanket, and rode bareback. The bridle was a rope around the horse's neck, then looped over his nose—just a hackamore. We had another rope, and used that to drag bundles of branches back to camp. For the first time in my life I felt important and useful.

We children had a play tepee made for us out of Gold Medal flour sacks, and I have a photograph of myself at age six standing in the doorway of the tepee and receiving a visit from Bear Head and another old Indian gentleman. Actually, they aren't paying much attention to me and are talking to each other in Blackfoot, but I felt highly honored anyway.

I should explain, lest everyone think I am imagining all this, that in those days my father used to take snapshots as field notes to record his trips. He had an old-fashioned Kodak, the kind with a bellows in front, and he was pretty skillful at taking pictures when nobody was noticing.

Back in San Francisco some years later, he and my stepmother, Dorothea Lange, gave me a small album called *Consie's Travel Book* which included pictures of an earlier trip to Arizona in 1915, along with some forty-one pictures of the Montana trip.

Among the best of the photographs of the Blackfoot, their tepees, and their life are pictures of Two Guns White Calf branding horses in a corral, another of visitors from a different encampment who came for the Brave Dog Society ceremonials, and one of Mary Two Guns and me playing with a puppy dog. There is one especially amusing photograph, simply titled *Saddle Horse*, showing a big blazed-faced roan with a fancy blanket thrown over him with cottonwood trees behind. In the middle foreground is the back of my father's easel with a large canvas on it; sketch box and other equipment are on the ground. It is easy to tell who took this photo: my father's shadow, Stetson hat and all, is clearly visible in the lower left foreground.

But somebody took a picture of my father painting up in the mountains. The big, jagged peaks in the background could only be the Rockies. Some kind of dark conifers are on the right side of the picture. My father has his easel set up at the base of the trees and his sketch box is open. His face is shadowed by his Stetson, and he holds his palette in his right hand. ("Gee, Mr. Dixon, how can you paint with your left hand?" So many people asked him this that it got to be a family joke.)

Maynard and Constance Dixon
c. 1921
by Dorothea Lange

He had an ingenious old sketch box, with places for palette, turpentine cup, brushes, tubes of oil paint, etc.; it also had slots in the cover to slide wet sketches into so they wouldn't touch anything and get smeared before the oil paint dried.

These sketches—actually small paintings—were his notes for future work in his studio. Many of them were very beautiful, painted with a verve and actuality that make them vibrant. As he said himself, most were "painted down the arm," by which I think he meant that his reflexes took over and he was painting almost automatically. But by 1917, there were years and years of experience behind him.

But finally, sometime in October, the snow came. It was a light, dry snow, powdery on the ground, but with it came cold weather. We had to go. My last memory of Montana is of sitting on the tailgate of a wagon and looking back at the wobbly lines of black made across the snow by the wagon wheels. It broke my heart. I wanted to stay and become an Indian.

Sign Talk
1917

Oil, 26″ x 30″

Private Collection

Home of the Blackfeet
1938

Oil, 30″ x 40″

Collection of the Cowboy Hall of Fame
Oklahoma City, Oklahoma

The Story Teller
Daniel Dixon

I remember my father best from the time when I was a small boy. And many of my memories are flavored by what he knew about the Indian and by what he felt about Indian ways.

Wrought into the silver head of his ebony sword cane was his personal and professional signature— a Navajo thunderbird.

He smoked an aromatic Indian herb called *kinni-kinnick,* which he rolled into cigarettes from packets of blue paper.

He could read the mood of the weather or the character of a landscape through eyes that always seemed to squint toward horizons, even in the cool gray fog of San Francisco.

He could sing the songs of the Navajo and the Blackfoot.

Sometimes, at the edge of a desert stream, he would bend willow branches into an Indian sweat lodge. When the framework was tied in place, he covered it with a tarpaulin. Then he heated rocks in a pit gouged out of the earth in the center of the lodge. Inside, we sat naked on juniper boughs and sprinkled water on the rocks, ash-white and splitting with heat. Steam rose in a hissing cloud, coaxing black streaks of grime from our pores and incense from the fragrant juniper.

In Taos, when I was six years old, he once gave me a gentle Indian pony of my own. No bridle, no saddle—I had to ride that pinto as the Indians did, and learned to make it my friend as well as my servant.

Later, in San Francisco, he set up an authentic tepee for the neighborhood kids to use as a clubhouse.

Above all, he was at home with silence and with solitude. Walking with him to the streetcar or sitting with him at the dinner table, there were times that I sensed him to be far away, alone in an immensity.

These gifts and understandings made my father seem rare and marvelous. But to me, his small son, he was most extraordinary of all when I went to visit his studio at 728 Montgomery Street.

The studio was on the top floor, two long flights up, at the back of the building. It was a single room about 30 feet long and 20 feet wide. Overhead a skylight tilted north. The walls were decorated with Indian rugs and blankets and baskets, a feathered Arapaho war bonnet, and two or three of my father's paintings—bold visions of Western sky, cloud, mountain, and mesa. Over the

728 Montgomery Street Studio
c. 1925

door, mounted in a blue circle, was a bleached buffalo skull. The air was sharp with the tang of paint, turpentine, and *kinni-kinnick.*

By the time I arrived, my father was usually ready to quit for the day. I waited while he cleaned his brushes and scraped his palette. Then, when he'd finished this ritual, he began another. "What kind of a story do you want today?" my father would ask. "I don't know. Any kind. Cowboys?"

"All right, cowboys," my father said. He went to the corner, lifted a booted foot, and toppled a cylinder of brown butcher paper. Another kick rolled it across the floor, leaving several feet of paper behind. My father took a box of colored crayons and got down on his hands and knees. I squatted beside him. He squinted at me over his glasses. "Injuns, too?" he asked. "Sure, Injuns!"

Then my father would tell me one of his stories. Sometimes it was an Indian myth or legend. Sometimes it came out of the history books—a tale about Kit Carson or the Pony Express or the great warrior Geronimo. Sometimes it was an account of his own journeys into the far places of the Southwest—expeditions that lasted up to several months, and that had taken him on horseback as far as Montana and to Mexico.

And as he spoke, my father illustrated his narrative on the brown butcher paper. His thin left wrist turned, color jumped out of his fingers, and suddenly his words became living things. Cowpunchers, trappers in buckskins, Mexican *vaqueros,* Indians hooded in robes or naked in the sun. Dusty horned toads, lizards and rattlesnakes, soaring eagles, coyotes and wolves, grizzly bears, deer and buffalo, longhorns and mustangs. Log cabins with flat sod roofs, tents and tepees, adobe *ranchos,* false-fronted saloons and stores. And all of this set in one uninterrupted landscape—sky, sun and shadow, clouds massed for thunderstorms, sagebrush and alkali dwindling into the distance, red rimrock, junipers and poplars and cottonwoods, rivers and little streams in green valleys. Wherever the story led, there was no break in the horizon. Here flowed into there, now into then, event into memory, and all things were related.

When my father had finished his story, he would tear it off the roll of brown butcher paper, circle it with a rubber band, and give it to me for my collection. They're gone now, those stories, all of them, God knows where. But my father's work remains, and so does his presence—a presence that, to a small boy, was as proud, as lonely, and as mysterious as the robed figures he painted against the red mesas, under an infinite sky.

Five Tonto Apaches
1900

Pencil, 11″ x 7″

Collection of Edith Hamlin

Robed Indian
N.D.

Pastel, 18″ x 11″

Private Collection

Robed Indian
N.D.

Pastel, 18″ x 11″

Recapturing the Spirit
John Dixon

One stormy morning in May of 1979, Andrew Maynard Dixon, my youngest son, Lisa Dixon, my only daughter, and I, piled into an undersized Japanese pickup truck and headed over the Sierra.

During that wonderful week we made a sweep across Nevada, Southern Utah, and Northern Arizona into the Navajo country, and to Monument Valley. Although I had never been to that area before, in spirit I felt I had been there many times. The landscape wasn't strange or unfamiliar. Some of my earliest childhood recollections involved this country and its people; when I visited my father's studio in San Francisco at 728 Montgomery Street, the walls and floors were covered, it seems, with the artifacts of those people, Indian blankets, pots, leggings, all sorts of things he had brought back from his painting expeditions to their land. He would tell us stories that he had written and at one time had published. "Injun Babies," they were called, full of mysticism, and scary to young people. I dimly remember an Indian "chief" from whom I learned an Indian song that I still remember. I've been lucky . . . very lucky. I feel that I know this country and I feel that I know the people. Not in an anthropological sense, but in a spiritual sense I think I know them. All of this I've absorbed from my father, from his great love of the people and the country, and from observing him paint and draw.

A Pacific storm that had chased us over the Sierra and across Nevada caught us the day we finally arrived in Monument Valley. The clouds were low and black and it was late in the afternoon, raining here, hailing there, and snowing elsewhere. The sun began to set under the clouds, and there in the strong, late afternoon light was Mitten Butte, just as it was in the small painting dated 1909, I think, that had hung in my boyhood room for years.

From Monument Valley to Hovenweep to Capitol Reef and back toward Zion National Park we went, through Panguitch, Utah arriving at Orderville after dark. The lady at the motel thought we were daft to be going down to Zion at night. "Can't see anything," she said. But the moon was full, and the skies had cleared, and I knew better. We approached the Park from the upper road. The ranger station was dark and empty, and as we passed through the forms and shapes of upper Zion, alone on the road, I turned off the motor and lights and we quietly rolled along, saying little, stopping here and there to drink in the glory of the place. As we approached the entrance to the long tunnel, there before us was *Moonlight Over Zion;* the same bright star was there, the quiet was there, the peace was there, and Espirito Maynardo was unmistakably there.

Zion is a special place for me. In the summer of 1940, we camped near the mouth of the main canyon. One of the most vivid memories I have of being with my father is of a warm summer afternoon at the Temple of Sinewava, a beautiful place in the canyon at a bend of the Virgin River. I remember my dad setting up his painting equipment, the smell of turpentine, the warm, gentle breeze that stirred the cottonwoods in the afternoon, and my first attempt at "serious" painting. I still have that first painting. It has in it the unmistakable touch of Maynard Dixon. I know, because he gave me a little help. The colors aren't right, but the shapes are good, and I can see his hand in them.

The next morning at Mt. Carmel, I was standing at the gate of the driveway leading to the familiar log house that Dad and Edie had built in 1940. It was their refuge from the summer heat of Tucson, Arizona. Surprisingly, after 30 years absence I found it unchanged. We spent summer vacations together there during the war years of 1941 through 1946. Occasionally, my brother Dan, my half-brother Ross, my sister Consie, and Edie's nieces, Carol and Joan, visited. The log cabin lay within a sheltered cove at the base of a range of juniper-studded hills. A small irrigation ditch followed the contours of the hills and gave rise to the usual stand of thirsty cottonwoods, silver maples, and Lombardy poplars. A gently curving gravelled driveway skirted the edge of a small meadow. Sagebrush surrounded all. The house contained a living room, kitchen, bath, bedroom, and sleeping loft. It had plenty of windows and up-to-date conveniences and was built of notched logs, the spaces between chinked with a coral clay plaster. There was a grape arbor built of poles at the rear of the house, and a garage nearby. There was a "real" one-room log cabin. Beyond the cabin was the Blackfoot tepee which Dad had brought back from Montana in 1917.

These were happy times. Maynard was not yet enslaved by an oxygen bottle, and although not active, was still able to work. Edie, bless her, was plenty active. Sometimes out of sheer exasperation Maynard would sing out, "Edie, for God's sake, sit down." She might, for a moment, but there was a great deal for her to do. And with her seemingly boundless energy she would soon be up and running.

Maynard was still able to go on occasional painting sorties, and on these occasions we would pack up some "grub," pile into the station wagon and be off through the sagebrush and juniper to a suitable spot facing the grand line of the white and vermillion cliffs. Out would come the camp stools and sketch boxes, Maynard and Edie often working side by side. I never tired of watching him paint, that thin figure, chest working hard to get enough breath, slender, almost delicate hands, the veins lying in rivers. On his head was the old black Stetson, in his mouth maybe a roll-your-own. He worked at a distance from his canvas, his figure erect, his left hand holding the brush or pencil. He worked quickly, with great economy of motion, blue eyes squinting, even in the late afternoon light. The image on the canvas board would begin to take form like a slow motion Polaroid.

The Enemy's Country
1942

Tempera, 13¼″ x 10¾″

Collection of Sara and Dean Hauter

Desert Ranges
1940

Oil, 25″ x 30″

C.R. Smith Collection
Huntington Art Gallery
University of Texas

There were quiet moments. I can still see him clearly, sitting in a camp chair, smoking his fragrant blend, holding the cigarette between thumb and forefinger with those expressive hands, maybe reading, writing letters, or sketching. It's not important what he was doing; he was there. And I remember the filtered sunlight, the warm dry air, the fragrance of his smoke, the peace and contentment. After Maynard died, Edie put a bronze plaque on a boulder that sits on the low ridge above the house.

These are some of the memories and impressions of Mt. Carmel that went flooding through my mind as I stood there at the gate in 1979 with my son and daughter. I picked a bunch of sagebrush which grew near the gate and brought it home with me. I don't know when I'll get back there again.

I spent some time with him at the winter place, an adobe house on the desert north of Tucson. I remember him working on the drawings for the limited edition of Parkman's *Oregon Trail*. Besides Edie, his constant companion in those times was the oxygen bottle which he lived with day and night. Still he worked, a gleam in his eye, the humor still there, even if the vigor wasn't. He was full of new ideas, new projects, and would talk about new directions toward which his work might go.

I am sitting here in my office, trying to be a writer. On the wall near me is a pen and ink drawing, inscribed "Bad Man for John, November 26, '39," a marvelous drawing of a lean-faced hombre, with a walrus moustache, peering with one cold eye from beneath the shadow of a Stetson, a bandana around his neck. I treasure it dearly. For me it is "Western Art" at its best. Next to it on the wall is a sketch in pencil of a jagged, dark mountain range, silhouetted against a storm-clouded sky, dated July 1945. It's a working reference drawing with notes at the bottom of the page that suggest his poetic nature. I especially treasure this drawing because although I know I probably wasn't with him when he made it, I like to think I was.

Maynard Dixon in San Francisco Studio
1937
by Sonya Noskowiak

Apache Acorn Gatherers
1915

Oil, 20″ x 30″

Courtesy of Rosenstock Arts
Denver, Colorado

Katchina Maker
1923

Oil, 16″ x 12″

Private Collection

Remembrances of a Friend
Winona Tomanoczy

San Franciscans of the 20s and 30s were accustomed to occasional glimpses of a tall, lean figure in distinctive Old West garb; black Stetson, silver-tipped ebony cane, narrow black pants and jacket, white shirt, knit tie, and polished cowboy boots. He might have been the reincarnation of Owen Wister's *Virginian*.

One morning in 1920, as I waited for the Union Street cable car, I overheard a waiter from the Black Cat Restaurant call out, "Morning, Mr. Dixon. Cold fog." "Cold as Christian charity," was the response of the man with the Western look, as he climbed the steep stairway leading to his third floor studio at 728 Montgomery, an address he was to make famous. That man was Maynard Dixon, popular Western artist and well known member of the Bohemian art group of that day.

Shortly thereafter, I was invited to a tea by Dorothea Lange to announce her engagement. The tea was held in her photographic portrait studio on Sutter near Powell, back of the old Hill Tolerton print rooms. One entered her spacious studio through a charming little patio with wall fountain and flowers. I heard the usual vivacious chatter and laughter of such occasions even though it was Prohibition time.

Dorothea greeted me saying, "Nonie, I want you to meet Maynard Dixon, the man I am going to marry. Maynard, this is a friend, Winona McCullough, Indian-Irish." I immediately recognized the tall, lean figure, half reclining on a floor cushion in front of the fireplace, as the man I had heard exchange greetings with the Black Cat waiter. He was rolling a Bull Durham cigarette with one hand—an accomplishment of which he seemed inordinately proud—and extended the other long fingered hand with a surprisingly firm grip. (I was later to learn that he was ambidextrous.)

He half murmured, with the characteristically quizzical grin I came to know well, "Winona, Child of the Forest," a term that was to become a familiar greeting throughout our long friendship—a friendship deepened by Maynard and Dorothea's marriage and the birth of their two sons, Daniel Rhodes and John Eaglefeather, both of whom became my godsons.

Throughout the years, both households moved in a periphery around Russian Hill, purely by chance choosing neighboring homes. Although our lives followed different channels—theirs in the art world, mine in public school education—we shared much of our social life and many friendships.

One of my friends was Paul Tomanoczy, who was later to become my husband. Paul was a violinist, linguist, former American Consul to his native Budapest, and owner of the old Civic Center Bookshop across from the Civic Auditorium. Maynard was already a personality in Western painting—he had deep knowledge of American Indian culture, as well as respect for the Old West and its rugged mountains and plains.

Maynard Dixon c. 1925
by George Hurrell

I thought Paul had raised a quizzical eyebrow when I pointed out Maynard in a crowd. Paul said lightly: "The great American myth. The West that never was. The noble savage versus the cruel scalper. The Buffalo Bill hero, the cowboy boots and the dashing Stetson." I was afraid Paul would think Maynard a bit of a *poseur.* They acknowledged my introduction with some formality but were soon matching wits and limericks. Then they made an engagement to see some of Maynard's book illustrations at the Grabhorn Press.

A few days later, while I was visiting Paul at his bookshop, I heard him say to an unseen visitor on the mezzanine floor, "I find myself using the phrase, 'a basic nobility in this man', and I do not use the word 'nobility' casually." When the visitor had gone, I learned that Paul had been speaking of Maynard. They developed a strong friendship, lunched occasionally, discussed books, art, the journalistic myths of the Old West, and puzzled over the confusion of "nice women" in the distinction between eroticism and pornography.

When Poppa Coppa's son reopened the old Red Paint Restaurant, a favorite of North Beach Bohemians during the Depression years, the walls were hung with paintings by various artists who had literally painted for their suppers—and one of Maynard's works was among them. The owner invited Maynard to take a table on Friday nights, seating perhaps a dozen guests, to help bring back the old conviviality.

Paul Tomanoczy escorted me there on a night I especially remember. Among those present were Harold von Schmidt, whom I then knew only as an illustrator for the *Saturday Evening Post;* Albert Elkus, head of the University of California's Music Department; Roi Partridge and Imogen Cunningham, etcher and photographer; Kem Weber, a designer of furniture for Barker Brothers; Hazel Dreiss, bookbinder for the Grabhorn Press; and Albert ("Mickey") Bender, an especially good friend and prominent patron of the arts.

It was during this period that Maynard seems to have developed a meaningful friendship with the distinguished composer, Ernest Bloch, who occasionally played for him in his studio. Coincidentally, Maynard had been reading the just-published Robinson Jeffers volume of poetry, *The Roan Stallion.* I was aware that Maynard was sinking into one of the periods of depression to which he was subject. Following an afternoon of music with Bloch and an evening of reading Jeffers' dark poetry, I could see he was in a real "slough of despond." It happened that he and Bloch had engaged in a long, philosophic, ultimately controversial discussion over what constitutes responsibility: the degree to which an artist, a genuinely creative artist, would be obligated to sacrifice his art for family and society.

Study for **Shapes of Fear**
1930

Charcoal and Red Crayon, 19¼″ x 24″

Collection of Edith Hamlin

Ute Indian
1933

Charcoal and Pastel, 27″ x 22″

Private Collection

Maynard felt that Bloch had condemned as escapism his long absences from family, studio, and career obligations for his ever-pressing need for sun and solitude. He had maintained to Bloch that his experiences in the rugged mountains and deserts—on ranches of the Old West with horses, wranglers, cowboys; his life with the many Indian tribes, sharing their tribal customs, studying their rituals and religions, learning their languages and their crafts—were the very foundations that made possible his career as an artist. Maynard believed and believed deeply.

Remembering this, I relive a moving experience when I look at what I think is my all-time favorite painting, Maynard Dixon's *Shapes of Fear,* in which he expressed his feeling about the Great Depression. Even the original color sketch still moves me. At the annual San Francisco Art Association exhibition in the Palace of the Legion of Honor (1932), *Shapes of Fear* won the Ranger Award. The San Francisco Annual was hung toward the closing of the city's first important Vincent Van Gogh exhibition. As Maynard and I were walking toward the Van Gogh room, I congratulated him on his award. He looked around, said slyly half-whispering, "But Winona, it also won the San Francisco popularity vote. I must be slipping."

Maynard fell silent as we entered the Van Gogh Gallery. He stopped before the famous *Bedroom at Arles.* In an emotional voice, he said, "I who came to scoff remain to pray. I could never really understand this man Van Gogh until this show. The humility, the simplicity, that only the truly great could see in a simple peasant bed, chair, patchwork quilt." He had tears in his eyes. I, too, was almost in tears. I realized that only an artist perceptive enough to have painted *Shapes of Fear* could have entered into the significance of Van Gogh's simplicity.

Maynard could be complex and unpredictable. One example was the furor caused by the construction of the Golden Gate Bridge. Maynard's brother-in-law was Charles Duncan, the public relations expert representing Joseph Strauss, the chief engineer of the Golden Gate Bridge Project. The Bridge was a subject of endless controversy among the San Francisco artists. Many visualized it as man's ultimate violation of the natural rugged grandeur of the Strait. To others, it promised to be one of man's crowning achievements in developing an important natural resource by use of twentieth century technology.

Maynard held a "pro-and-con powwow" in his studio. Strauss and Duncan were present with maps, models, and technology to present their case. A few of the artists were for the bridge, but the majority were against the entire project. Maynard, the great protagonist of an unspoiled world, surprisingly enough leaned toward the "pro." After a prolonged and heated discussion, the meeting ended with an agreement to make no protest at that time to the bridge authorities.

In 1939, Maynard's failing health in San Francisco's foggy climate dictated his resolve to make one more trip to his beloved desert and mountains. He had emphysema complicated with asthma. We all knew this was to be his last trip from the city he loved. He and his dedicated wife, Edith Hamlin, held a sale extraordinary in the history of San Francisco art.

They did a tremendous job of cataloging and classifying Maynard's drawings, easel paintings, architectural designs, and mural sketches. Never had San Franciscans witnessed such a demonstration of one artist's popularity. They were all there: fellow artists and artisans; art patrons coveting just "one more Dixon" for their private collections; fellow Bohemian Club members; and devotees of the Old West. It seemed as if all San Franciscans wanted this last chance to buy a Dixon, any Dixon they could pay for. From the procceds of the sale, Maynard and Edith were able to buy a Ford station wagon, build the new adobe house they were to live in on the desert outside Tucson, and shortly thereafter, the lodge at Mt. Carmel, Utah. San Francisco was a little less for their leaving.

Finally and paradoxically, Maynard Dixon comes through the welter of words written about him as a striking individual, at once his own man—a quiet, even taciturn, personality and a witty social being. He was equally at home at a formal museum opening night, at a gala Bohemian Club dinner, or in his prized life of desert solitude among his Indian friends. My own life was enriched for having known him. Maynard Dixon was well worth knowing.

Studies for
Hopi Men
Hopi Women
1925

Tempera, 40″ x 14″

Private Collections

Migration
1924

Oil, 20″ x 30″

Private Collection

The Later Years:
A Tribute to Maynard
Edith Hamlin

Taking a long look backward, I remember clearly my first awareness of Maynard Dixon and his paintings. During my art school days, 1920 to 1924, at the California School of Fine Arts, I was attracted to his striking Southwestern landscapes exhibited at the local Beaux Arts or Gump galleries. With my own interest in landscape study, his distinctive style, color, and design were especially appealing, and even then, I think, I was half in love with the Southwest, from those Dixon canvases. Maynard was easily identifiable, striding down Post Street near the galleries in his usual Stetson hat and old-style boots. Little did I imagine that thirteen years later he would become a valued friend, and even later my husband.

Returning in 1933 to the Bay Area after some years in New York, I re-entered the San Francisco art scene as a professional artist. My first objective was to take part in the 1930s renaissance in mural programs sponsored by the Public Works Art Project and later the Works Project Administration. Meantime I had married a fellow artist and photographer, Albert Barrows. The art community was then a smaller, close-knit community; and despite the Depression, there was a stimulating atmosphere from the art activity sponsored by the government, including economic aid.

My first meeting with Maynard was through my husband, Albert, who knew him, and also Albert's fellow photographer, Dorothea Lange. Maynard became one of a small group of artists who gathered weekly in our spacious Montgomery Street studio, where Albert held a class in "Space Division," his own mathematic version of Jay Hambidge's "Dynamic Symmetry" system for visual composition in the arts. At that time I was impressed with Maynard's personality, intelligence, and humor. Soon after, the Dixon-Lange marriage ended, and Maynard came to live in his studio nearby at 728 Montgomery Street. It was a sad and difficult time for Maynard. Albert and I visited with him occasionally in our Montgomery Street studio, or in his own close by.

Meantime, my own brief marriage came to an abrupt end, about a year after Maynard's. At that time I was developing the working-drawings for my two Mission High School murals; Maynard was very helpful in his critiques, especially for the sketches of the Indian figures in the murals. He reciprocated by asking for my opinions on his works-in-progress in his studio. I remember vividly having tea in his studio with the Kit Carson murals underway as a backdrop, and sharing an aromatic dinner tray brought up from nearby Chinatown. His old studio, as well as mine (which had a fireplace!) hold many cherished memories. Maynard's painting took on renewed creativity, and my tempera murals prospered. I'm sure that our mutually bereft situations following divorce ("washed up on the same beach" we called it) was one initial element in our attraction. In any event, it was not only a consoling but a very companionable time. Aside from his "batching" in his studio, Maynard would also frequently enjoy my Telegraph Hill cottage—his "part-time home" he called it.

**Edith Hamlin and
Maynard Dixon**

During the years from 1935 to 1940, there were many changes in Maynard's life. There was an extended stay in and around Carson City, Nevada, where the Dixon-Lange divorce was secured. Maynard, despite his loneliness and depression, produced several major compositions and many fresh field-sketch paintings. *Shorelines of Lahontan,* with its geometric Indian-like pattern, is a masterpiece. Returning to his San Francisco studio, he then designed and executed the Kit Carson murals.

In the summer of 1937, Maynard with his two young sons, Daniel and John, accompanied by a fellow artist who drove the old station wagon, set forth on a painting and camping trip. Crossing the deserts of Nevada and going as far as the high plains of Wyoming, the trip held drama as well as good sketch material. The old car developed a broken axle during a stormy desert crossing and later, much to the boys' delight, they took in a riotous Indian and cowboy rodeo, complete with drunken characters. Maynard made only a few catch-as-catch-can Shoshone Indian sketches in the Wind River country, and brought back a good group of landscape studies. Two of the outstanding studio compositions drawn from this excursion were *Cloud-Drift and Prairie (page 91),* and *Wind of Wyoming.*

After his return from this trip, Maynard and I decided to "tie the knot." Quietly slipping off to Carson City, the car loaded with painting and camping supplies, we headed over the Sierra to our destination. When telling his sons goodbye, they asked, "Where are you headed for, Dad?" He answered, with a twinkle in his eye, "I'm off to Carson to buy a new hat." Our September marriage took place on the spacious veranda of the historic Bliss-Yerington mansion of some Carson City friends. We lingered there through October under serene fall skies and autumn color. Maynard was a remarkably creative and youthful man for his sixty-two years.

During the following two years, the Dixon-Hamlin alliance held both success and misfortune. Often we were away from our Telegraph Hill cottage and studios for many months on painting expeditions into the Southwest, but would return for mural commissions and studio work. In 1939 Maynard completed one of his major mural commissions, *The Indian Yesterday* and *The Indian Today,* for the new offices of the Bureau of Indian Affairs in Washington, D.C.

Eventually we were able to make our long-planned migration to Tucson in late 1939. From the joys and peace of our new life under the Arizona sun, Maynard was granted seven more creative years. The sunny patio of the adobe home on the desert near Tucson had the same authentic style, serenity, and peace expressed in Maynard's earlier Taos painting, *Como Se Pasa la Vida (page 34).* It was our home-place refuge and was dear to our hearts. During those years, we also built a log and stone house for the summer and fall months at Mt. Carmel, Utah. In a land of bright mesas, pioneer villages, and seasonal color, it was a painter's paradise. Despite the allure of the Paiute,

The Medicine Robe
1915

Oil, 40" x 30"

Collection of the Whitney Gallery of Western Art
Buffalo Bill Historical Center
Cody, Wyoming

Cloud-Drift and Prairie
1940

Oil, 30″ x 40″

Collection of Dr. R.V.A. Lee

Hopi, and Navajo lands nearby, Maynard's painting trips there were necessarily limited. Those mile-high locations affected his breathing, already restricted by emphysema. Nevertheless, his memories of the Native Americans were presented in some outstanding canvases of the early forties; *Land of the White Mesas* is one of these paintings.

Beginning in 1939, we came to know some of the Papago in Tucson. At the nearby San Xavier Mission and Reservation, the old-time wattled huts and adobe dwellings with ramada shelters were incorporated in Maynard's field sketches. He made portrait studies and sketches of Papago horsemen and cowboys. The annual Papago Fair and Indian Rodeo was always a festive event at Sells. Two of our special new friends were Gwyneth, an anthropologist, and her Papago husband, Juan Xavier. Maynard and Juan developed a *simpatico* friendship, and Juan would sit for us for portrait studies. We spent memorable evenings at the Xaviers' simple adobe home near the Mission where we shared Indian-style suppers, good talk and Papago songs. The Yaqui village of Pascua near Tucson, where this transplanted Mexican tribal group had settled, also provided colorful experiences. Here we witnessed the Pascola celebrations at Easter time, which included the Deer Dance and other ceremonial dances. Maynard's return to the Southwest in these later years was a cherished dream come true. His life-long love of the "Sunland," its starkly bold deserts and ranges, the pioneer and native people, gave him fulfillment.

In 1942, a commission of special interest was offered to Maynard. The Limited Editions Club of New York asked him to illustrate a deluxe edition of Francis Parkman's *Oregon Trail*. This classic historical account of Parkman's journey among the Plains Indians and Mountain Men in 1846 was a tale dear to Maynard's heart. He was uniquely qualified to illustrate this work and spent many months upon the assignment. The fifty-five pen and ink drawings scattered through the text, and the eight pages in color, as well as end pages and cover design, made it a distinguished volume. All of the one thousand or so books were sent to him to sign.

I sometimes have been asked for my opinion as to which periods in Maynard's career I consider high points in his creative output. I can only answer this: in general, each of several progressions in his career have outstanding works. For instance, from 1912 to the late 1920s, he became, in his own and other's opinions, a "fine art" artist, rather than primarily an "illustrator." Excellent works from that period are *The Medicine Robe (page 90)*, *Mystery Stone (page 22)*, and *The Trail to Pei-ki-hat-tsoh (page 43)*. During the 1920s, as his work became less Post-Impressionist, his canvases evolved into a more characteristic style marked by bold light-and-dark patterns and carefully planned "space division" composition. Outstanding paintings of that period include *The Circle of Shimaikuli (page 26)*, *The Wise Men (page 15)*, *The Ancients (page 9)*, and *Cloud World (page 27)*. The mural hanger for the Arizona Biltmore Hotel, *Legend of Earth and Sun* was also important.

The 1930s were also undoubtedly a rich period for the artist. Outstanding canvases were *Earth Knower, Men of the Red Earth (page 39), Shorelines of Lahontan,* and *Cloud-Drift and Prairie (page 91),* Perhaps this could be considered another peak period for Maynard's career.

Considering his failing health, it is remarkable that during the last years of Maynard's life, from 1940 to the time of his death, he produced excellent canvases: *Canyon Ranch (Utah), Desert Ranges (California) (page 75),* and two Arizona subjects, *Drought and Downpour,* and *Home of the Desert Rat.*

In the final two or three years when the battle for enough oxygen had become crucial, Maynard developed studio pursuits to suit his waning energy. He perfected his watercolor technique through a series of Western ranch subjects, entertaining himself by commenting on the Arizona "dude" ranch scene. But there were times when he became discouraged and restive, when his still creative spirit felt thwarted by his physical limitations. I remember him remarking, "I don't want to continue producing works in the same manner—I need a whole new direction." At such times he turned to writing or to reading. One wonders what he might have produced given more time and the vital breath of life. His moving to Tucson allowed him to continue a dream of the land and people of the Southwest. To paint and draw was an ideal with him and almost a trust that he should present the West in a way that was true to his deeper feelings, in a way few other artists had chosen.

We had a very good life, really, for which I am grateful.

Edith Hamlin

Visionary

Am I a fool
in that I am deep-willed to seek
always a vision
known never to be reached.
Yet, so having striven,
having crushed my heart (and yours)
against the hard will of the world,
and though determination has grown gaunt
with an immortal hunger,
I am not yet resigned to wait.
I am deep-willed to strive
so that if old age, or even death,
only make answer
I still can say
out of all the intense devotion of a soul
somehow here I have created beauty.

Maynard Dixon, 1923

Maynard Dixon,
Tucson, Arizona 1945
by Ansel Adams

Bibliography

Books and Monographs

Burnside, Wesley M. *Maynard Dixon, Artist of the West.*
Provo: Brigham Young University Press. 1974.

California Historical Society. *Rim-Rock and Sage: the
Collected Poems of Maynard Dixon with Drawings.* San
Francisco, 1977.

Hagerty, Donald J., Interviewer and Editor. *Edith Hamlin— A
California Artist* (Oral History). American Studies Program,
University of California, Davis. 1981.

Hassrick, Peter H. *The Way West: Art of Frontier America.*
New York: Harry N. Abrams, Inc., 1977.

Meltzer, Milton. *Dorothea Lange, A Photographer's Life.* New
York: Farrar Strauss Giroux. 1978.

Oakland Museum. *Celebrating a Collection— the Work of
Dorothea Lange.* Oakland. 1978.

Taylor, Joshua. *America as Art.* Washington, D.C.:
Smithsonian Institution Press. 1976.

Wallace, Grant. *Maynard Dixon: Painter and Poet of the Far
West.* San Francisco Art Research Project, Works Project
Administration. 1937. (Versions "A" and "B")

Periodicals and Articles

Dixon, Maynard. "Arizona in 1900." *Arizona Highways.*
February, 1942.

Dixon, Maynard. "Navajo Land." *Arizona Highways.* May,
1942.

Hamlin, Edith. "Maynard Dixon, Artist of the West."
California Historical Quarterly. Winter, 1974.

Lummis, Charles F. "A California Illustrator—Maynard
Dixon and His Work." *Land of Sunshine.* December, 1898.

Pielkovo, Ruth. "Dixon, Painter of the West." *International
Studio.* March, 1924.

Starr, Kevin. "Painterly Poet, Poetic Painter: the Dual Art of
Maynard Dixon." *California Historical Quarterly.* Winter,
1977/78.

Tolerton, Hill. "The Art of Maynard Dixon." *International
Studio.* May, 1915.

Newspapers

Los Angeles *Times.* August 2, 1913; April 9, 1933.
San Francisco *Examiner.* March 29, 1939; October 3, 1939.
Daily Californian. December 4, 1925.

Miscellaneous

Dane Coolidge Collection. Courtesy of the Bancroft Library.
Maynard Dixon Collection. Courtesy of the Bancroft Library.
Maynard Dixon Collection. Courtesy of Edith Hamlin.